Neighborhood Song

D0479271

Trish Holland

 TeachingStrategies® · Bethesda, MD

Copyright © 2010 by Teaching Strategies, LLC.

All rights reserved. No part of this publication may be reproduced or distributed in any form, or by any means, or stored in a database or retrieval system without the prior written permission of Teaching Strategies, LLC.

For Teaching Strategies, LLC.
Publisher: Larry Bram
Editorial Director: Hilary Parrish Nelson
VP Curriculum and Assessment: Cate Heroman
Product Manager: Kai-leé Berke
Book Development Team: Sherrie Rudick and Jan Greenberg
Project Manager: Jo A. Wilson

For Q2AMedia
Editorial Director: Bonnie Dobkin
Editor and Curriculum Adviser: Suzanne Barchers
Program Manager: Gayatri Singh
Creative Director: Simmi Sikka
Project Manager: Santosh Vasudevan
Designer: Ritu Chopra
Picture Researchers: Judy Brown & Stephanie Mills

Picture Credits
t–top b–bottom c–center l–left r–right

Cover: Jurgen Magg/Jupiter.

Back Cover: Keith Brofsky/Photolibrary.

Title page: Jurgen Magg/Jupiter.

Insides: Frances M Roberts/Photolibrary: 3, Keith Brofsky/Photolibrary: 4, Keith Levit Photography/Photolibrary: 5, Morgan Lane Photography/Shutterstock: 6, Masterfile: 7, Jupiter Images: 8, Mike Brake/Shutterstock: 9, Vadim Kozlovsky/Dreamstime: 10, Stephen Coburn/Dreamstime: 11l, Stephen Coburn/Dreamstime: 11r, Monkey Business Images Ltd./Photolibrary: 12, SW Productions/Photolibrary: 13t, Monkey Business Images Ltd./Photolibrary: 13b, Alex Mares-Manton/Photolibrary: 14, Stephen Coburn/Pam Ostrow/Jupiter Images: 15t, Avava/Dreamstime: 15b, Peter Bennett/Photolibrary: 16, Corbis/Jupiter Images: 17, Lisa F. Young/Shutterstock: 18, Mark Hunt/Photolibrary: 19, Jurgen Magg/Jupiter Images: 20, Ariell Skelley/Jupiter Images: 21, Rmarmion/Dreamstime: 22, Istockphoto: 23t, Robert Dowey/Photolibrary: 23b, Ryan McVay/Photolibrary: 24.

Teaching Strategies, LLC.
Bethesda, MD
www.TeachingStrategies.com

ISBN: 978-1-60617-143-1

Library of Congress Cataloging-in-Publication Data
Holland, Trish.
  Neighborhood song / Trish Holland.
     p. cm.
  ISBN 978-1-60617-143-1
  1. Neighborhoods--Juvenile literature. 2. Neighbors--Juvenile literature. I. Title.
  HM761.H65 2010
  307--dc22
                                    2009044287
CPSIA tracking label information:
RR Donnelley, Shenzhen, China
Date of Production: March 2018
Cohort: Batch 8

Printed and bound in China

    10 11 12   18
————————————   ————————
    Printing   Year Printed

This is the way we live together,
Live together, live together.
This is the way we live together
In our neighborhood.

This is the way we travel around,
Travel around, travel around.
This is the way we travel around
In our neighborhood.

This is the way we go to school,
Go to school, go to school.
This is the way we go to school
In our neighborhood.

These are the people who care for us,
Care for us, care for us.
These are the people who care for us
In our neighborhood.

This is the way we do our work,
Do our work, do our work.
This is the way we do our work
In our neighborhood.

This is the way we get our food,
Get our food, get our food.
This is the way we get our food
In our neighborhood.

This is the way we get our clothes,
Get our clothes, get our clothes.
This is the way we get our clothes
In our neighborhood.

This is the way we keep things nice,
Keep things nice, keep things nice.
This is the way we keep things nice
In our neighborhood.

This is the way we help our neighbors,
Help our neighbors, help our neighbors.
This is the way we help our neighbors
In our neighborhood.

This is the way we play together,
Play together, play together.
This is the way we play together
In our neighborhood.

This is the way we get together,
Get together, get together.
This is the way we get together
In our neighborhood.

This is the way we celebrate,
Celebrate, celebrate.
This is the way we celebrate
In our neighborhood.